250 WORLD WAR I FACTS FOR KIDS

INTERESTING EVENTS & HISTORY
INFORMATION TO WIN TRIVIA

SCOTT MATTHEWS

CONTENTS

ABOUT THE AUTHOR

 Scott Matthews is a geologist, world traveller and author of the 'Amazing World Facts' series! He was born in Brooklyn New York by immigrant parents from the Ukraine but grew up in North Carolina. Scott studied at Duke University where he graduated with a degree in Geology and History.

His studies allowed him to travel the globe where he saw and learned amazing trivial knowledge with his many encounters. With the vast amount of interesting information he accumulated he created his best selling books 'Random, Interesting & Fun Facts You Need To Know'.

He hopes this book will provide you with hours of fun, knowledge, entertainment and laughter.

If you gain any knowledge from this book, think it's fun and could put a smile on someone's face, he would greatly appreciate your review on Amazon.

7 BENEFITS OF READING FACTS

1. Knowledge
2. Stress Reduction
3. Mental Stimulation
4. Better Writing Skills
5. Vocabulary Expansion
6. Memory Improvement
7. Stronger Analytical Thinking Skills

In the midst of chaos, there is also opportunity.

— Sun Tzu

WWI Timeline

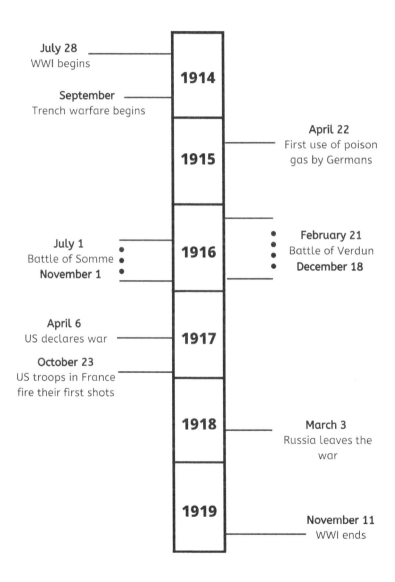

July 28
WWI begins

September
Trench warfare begins

1914

April 22
First use of poison
gas by Germans

1915

February 21
Battle of Verdun
December 18

July 1
Battle of Somme
November 1

1916

April 6
US declares war

October 23
US troops in France
fire their first shots

1917

1918

March 3
Russia leaves the
war

1919

November 11
WWI ends

250 FACTS

1) Right before the war, Europe was divided into two main alliances. The Triple Entente included Britain, Russia, and France. The Triple Alliance included Germany, Italy, and Austro-Hungary.

2) Italy went back on its word to the Triple Alliance when the war started, and it failed to join the war when it broke out in 1914.

3) In the decade leading up to WWI, Germany and Britain had a naval arms race. Britain won the race because it was able to acquire thirty-eight battleships while Germany only had twenty-four.

4) Before the war started in 1914, France and Russia had 928,000 more soldiers than Austro-Hungary and Germany. This means the Triple Entente had a numerical advantage over the Triple Alliance. Great Britain had a standing army of 248,000 which was very small compared to other major countries at the time.

5) The Balkan States (a collection of countries in Eastern Europe that included Greece, Serbia, Bulgaria, Macedonia, and Bosnia), were engaged in two consecutive wars in 1912 and 1913, and in the end, Serbia emerged as a nationalist state.

6) At the beginning of the war, Russia mobilized 5 million men, Germany mobilized 4.5 million men, France mobilized 3.8 million men, and Britain mobilized 0.75 million men.

7) Britain wanted to recruit 200,000 men in the first month of the war, but they surpassed their target when 300,000 men enlisted. Throughout the duration of the war, about 2.5 million Britons volunteered for the war, but only a quarter of them were eligible for enlistment.

British soldiers walking to Somme

8) When the war started in 1914, many in Britain thought that it would be over very soon, and those who joined the army expected that they would be home by Christmas.

9) Compulsory enlistment into the army was introduced in Britain in 1916. Roughly 750,000 British citizens appealed against compulsory enlistment in the first six months after it came into effect. Most of them were given temporary exemptions so that they could get their affairs in order before joining the army. Those who refused to fight out of principle, and for no other reason, were each given a white feather as a symbol of their cowardice.

10) In 1914, the British Empire had more than 400 million people, and Britain could bring in fighters from India and other territories.

11) 27% of all Scotsmen between the ages of fifteen and forty nine volunteered for the war before the end of 1915.

12) In 1917, The Russian Government started "Battalions of Death" that consisted entirely of female soldiers. These battalions were never put on the battlefront, but they were used to shame Russian male soldiers into fighting harder.

13) For the entire war, Germany mobilized 13.4 million men in total. This was the highest number of any country that took part in WWI.

14) The longest battle in the entire war was called the Battle of Verdun. It started in February 1916 and ended in December 1916, lasting more than 300 days. The bloodiest battle in the entire war was called The Battle of Somme. On the first day alone, Britain lost 60,000 troops. In total, Britain lost 460,000 men, France lost 200,000 men, and Germany lost 500,000 men.

15) When the war started in 1914, none of the armies

offered their soldiers equipment or uniforms that were designed to meet the demands of modern warfare. They all had colorful uniforms and soft hats, which made them easy targets in the battlefield. All countries adopted the use of steel helmets and camouflage outfits during the course of the war.

16) The use of trenches in WWI started in September 1914. Digging trenches was necessary because both sides had sophisticated machine guns that could fire 600 rounds per minute and mow down soldiers in open fields.

Trench warfare

17) Germany pioneered the use of flamethrowers in battle in February, 1915. Their flamethrowers could shoot jets of fire up to 130 feet (40 meters) long.

18) Military tanks were first used in battle on September 15, 1916, during what came to be called The Battle of Somme. Tanks were supposed to be called "land-ships," but Britain named them "tanks" in order to make

German spies think that they were building water tanks and not weapons.

19) Soldiers would often build mine shafts through no man's land in order to place and blow up explosives beneath enemy lines before major assaults. Some explosives used in the war were so loud they could be heard miles away. In 1917, explosives going off underneath German lines at Messines Ridge (Ypres) were heard 139 miles (225 kilometres) away in London.

20) Both sides used toxic gas during the war. 1.2 million soldiers were killed in gas attacks while many more were injured and disfigured.

Soldiers wearing gas masks

21) More than seventy different types of aircraft were used in WWI. At first, they were mostly used for spying on the enemy, but as the war progressed, they were increasingly used as fighters and bombers.

22) British whippet tanks were instrumental in the allies'

success near the end of the war because they were faster and more flexible than German machines.

23) The aviator term "dogfight" actually originated in WWI. Pilots had to switch off engines mid-air to keep the planes from stalling during sharp turns. The pilots noticed that when they restarted the engines, they sounded like barking dogs. As a result, mid-air confrontations with enemy pilots were named dog-fights.

24) Over twelve million letters were sent from Britain to France every week. Even during the war it only took two days for a letter to be delivered.

25) On May 7th, 1915, a German submarine attacked a civilian cruise line, killing roughly 1,200 people, 128 of whom were Americans. This influenced America's decision to join WWI on the side of the allies.

26) During WWI, German submarine (U-boat) attacks were so common in the Atlantic Ocean that 1.4 million tonnes of supplies shipped by the allies were sunk in a span of three months in late 1916. Germany constructed 360 submarine U-boats. Of those, 176 were destroyed during the war. German U-boat submarines managed to sink half of all British merchant ships in an effort to weaken the British economy during the war.

27) The greatest sea battle of WWI was called the Battle of Jutland. It took place from May 31st to June 1st, 1916. The fighting was so intense that the British navy lost fourteen battleships, while the German navy lost eleven battleships.

28) During WWI, it was almost impossible to navigate the North Sea because both sides of the conflict used heavy mines there. This was done in violation of a standing 1907 treaty that restricted the use of mines near an enemy's coastline.

29) The allies imposed a naval blockade of Germany from August 1914 to January 1919. This plan was very effective because Germany relied heavily on imports. Scholars estimate that 424,000 German lives were lost as a result of the blockade.

30) In Britain, more than 700,000 women were employed in factories that manufactured weapons during the war.

31) In Britain, there were about 16,000 soldiers who refused to fight for moral reasons. A few of them were put in non-combatant roles in the army, while the rest were sent to prison.

32) In all European countries, women and civilians who stayed home during the war died at very high rates because of malnutrition. Germany, in particular, experienced hundreds of thousands of deaths due to a combination of starvation and hunger-related illnesses.

33) Before WWI, it was rare for women to work in factories, but by the end of the war, between 36% - 37% of the industrial workforce in both France and Britain was female.

Women in munitions production factory

34) In Germany, turnips were considered animal feed until the winter of 1916, when they were used to feed people because of potato and meat shortages. That winter is still known as "Turnip Winter" in Germany. Similarly, meat became very scarce in Germany during the war. By the end of 1916, the meat supply had dropped to 31% compared to peacetime supply, and by the end of 1918, it had gone as low as 12%.

35) An Australian war hero named Private Billy Sing is credited with killing over 150 Turkish soldiers when he was a sniper during WWI. He earned the nickname "murderer" from his fellow soldiers.

36) A German pilot named Ernst Udet flew sixty one successful missions during WWI, making him one of the best pilots at the time.

37) A lone Portuguese soldier named Anibal Milhais was able to single-handedly withstand two German assaults. During the ongoing gunfight, he fought so hard that he

convinced the German soldiers that they were dealing with an entire army unit, instead of just one soldier.

38) A British nurse named Edith Cavell helped 200 allied soldiers escape from Belgium, which was occupied by Germany at the time.

39) A sixteen-year-old boy named John Cornwell was the youngest soldier to be awarded the Victoria Cross (a special medal issued to wounded allied soldiers). Despite getting a fatal wound, he held his post for over an hour.

40) Dogs had many crucial roles in the war, and they were used by both sides. Their roles included carrying supplies, locating wounded soldiers, sniffing out enemy positions, delivering messages across the battlefield, and companionship. About one million dogs lost their lives on the battlefield during WWI.

41) Homing pigeons were very important messengers during the war. In Britain, they even passed a law that would punish the killing, wounding or molesting of homing pigeons with up to six months of jail time. A homing pigeon named Cher Ami is credited with saving the lives of 194 American soldiers who were trapped behind enemy lines. Cher managed to reach her loft and deliver her message despite being shot through the chest and losing her vision in one eye.

42) A total of approximately eight million horses were killed in the war.

43) There were approximately 37.5 million casualties whose deaths were directly related to the WWI conflict.

Seven million soldiers were permanently injured or crippled for the rest of their lives after the war. It's estimated that 230 soldiers died every hour during WWI.

44) Shell shock was a common condition that affected soldiers on both sides of the war. 80,000 British servicemen suffered from shell shock as a result of the war. It was a mental condition that resulted from spending a lot of time on battlefields with intense artillery shelling.

45) The central powers spent $11,345 for every soldier they killed during WWI. The allies spent $36,486 for every soldier they killed.

46) To encourage support for the war back at home, Britain made and distributed war-themed toys, including toy tanks and toy soldiers.

47) An elephant named Lizzie was enlisted in the British army, and she was used to transport munitions into battle.

48) A Boston terrier bulldog named Stubby was trained to detect incoming shells before the soldiers could hear them. He would start barking, and soldiers would know that it was time to take cover. He was so good at his job that he officially earned the title Sergeant Stubby.

John Pershing awards Sergeant Stubby with a medal

49) Sometimes, cats were brought along to serve as mascots for various army units. One such example was Peter the cat, who accompanied a unit called the Northumberland Hussars.

50) Two out of every three Australian soldiers who went to fight in WWI didn't make it back home alive.

51) When WWI ended, 11% of all French people were either dead or wounded.

52) As a result of WWI, four whole empires collapsed. They included the Austro-Hungarian Empire, The Ottoman Empire, the Russian Empire, and the German Empire. Several modern countries including Estonia, Lithuania, Finland, Latvia, and Poland, rose as independent nations from the ashes of WWI.

53) When the war ended, Germany was forced to take responsibility for the whole war, and to pay $31.4 billion to the allies as compensation for damages and loss of life.

Adjusted for inflation, that's equivalent to $442 billion in today's cash.

54) Thirty different countries were directly involved in WWI.

55) When the British army started building tanks, they categorized them into female and male tanks. The female ones were fitted with machine guns, while the male ones were fitted with cannons.

56) The German army used terror tactics to keep civilians in occupied territories from rebelling. At one point, they shot 150 civilians in Belgium to show the rest that their orders were to be obeyed.

57) America refused to take sides at the start of WWI. Some American citizens who wanted to help the allies, took their own initiative and joined the French, Canadian, and British Armies.

58) US President Woodrow Wilson was re-elected in 1916 on a promise to keep America out of WWI. However, just one month after he was sworn in, he felt obligated to declare war on Germany.

59) America drafted 2.7 million men to join the US Army during WWI with an additional 1.3 million men volunteering later to join.

60) The Spanish Flu accounted for one third of all military deaths during WWI. It was very easy for soldiers to become sick because the trenches were extremely dirty and full of bacteria.

61) Even though the US was late in joining the allied war effort, it spent $30 billion during WWI.

62) Nine out of ten British soldiers survived when they were in the trenches. British soldiers rarely saw the firing lines during the war and were always moving around the trenches. This allowed them to keep away from the dangers of enemy fire.

63) Based on casualty figures, WWI is the sixth deadliest conflict in human history.

64) At the time, WWI was referred to by many different names, including "The World War," "The Great War," "The War to End All Wars," and "The War of the Nations."

65) Soldiers whose faces were disfigured during WWI often wore special masks to cover their wounds or scars. These masks only covered the disfigured parts of the face, and they were painted to look like the rest of the face.

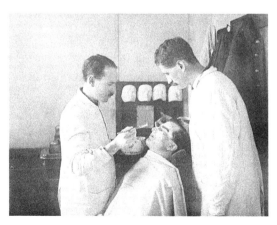

Soldier with facial injuries has a plaster cast made

66) Although most of the fighting occurred on European soil, the WWI conflicts spilled over to all oceans and all habitable continents in the world.

67) Three-quarters of all Russian soldiers who fought in the war were either killed, wounded or unaccounted for by the time Russia left the war.

68) German trenches were better constructed than British trenches. They were equipped with electricity, water taps, bunk beds, furniture, and some rooms even had doorbells.

69) In the case of gas attacks, soldiers on both sides of the conflict were trained to soak pieces of cloth in urine and hold them over their faces. It wasn't until 1918 that proper gas masks were provided to the soldiers.

70) During the war, the French developed a cannon that could shoot accurately up to 4 miles (about 6.4kms). The Germans feared it so much that they called it the "Devil Gun." French commanders believed that the allies won the war because of this one weapon.

71) When the US joined WWI, most moviegoers in America had to sit through four-minute pro-war speeches before they could watch any films.

72) American foods of German origin were renamed during WWI because people started to dislike German culture. Hamburgers became Salisbury steaks, dachshunds became liberty dogs, and frankfurters became liberty sausages.

73) 200,000 African Americans were enlisted in the Army during WWI. The army had segregated divisions so they

were trained separately. Only 11% of them were put in combat roles, while most of them were given manual labor roles. 13,000 Native Americans served in the US Military in WWI, although they were not granted US Citizenship until a few years after the war had ended.

74) Germans were very good at intercepting and breaking the codes used by the allies in the early stages of WWI. This continued until the United States decided to use lesser-known Native American languages for their coded messages. Members of the Choctaw tribe were put in charge of encoding messages, and from that point on, Germans couldn't translate any of the messages.

75) The United States became the world's greatest military power during WWI. The country underwent a broad military build-up as they prepared to join the war.

76) The Turks killed approximately 1.5 million Armenian civilians during WWI. This genocide went mostly unnoticed at the time because other countries were so busy fighting the war that they couldn't intervene or raise concerns.

77) WWI helped to fast-track the liberation of women. When men were off fighting the war, women took over many jobs that were reserved for men. By the time the war ended, it was clear to everyone that women were just as capable as men in the workplace. Older women in Britain were even given the right to vote before the war ended. The US granted women the right to vote in 1920, the year of the first major election after the war.

78) After WWI, Britain lost its leadership position in the

world economy because it had spent so much money and resources, lost so many people, and incurred heavy damages during the war.

79) The WWI trenches covered over 25,000 miles (40,000 kms). They started on the English Channel and extended all the way to Switzerland.

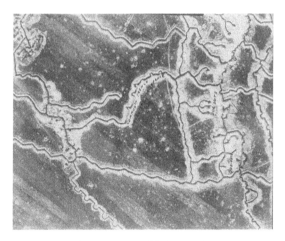

Aerial photograph of WWI trenches

80) When the war started, Britain cut all German undersea cables. That way, the allies were the only ones who were able to send quick messages to the United States.

81) Britain had a secret publication task force called The Wellington House during the war. It published war picture books in different languages and distributed them in major countries across the world. Those books helped to turn several countries (e.g. China) against Germany.

82) In 1917, President Woodrow Wilson created a

Committee on Public information which used many different tactics, including creating pro-war films, posters, pamphlets, adverts, and books to convince Americans to support the war. The committee also paid clergymen and professors to give pro-war sermons and lectures to people in churches and colleges.

83) Right after the war started, Germany was working on plans to turn Central and Western Europe into a common market that they would control to their benefit. This means that if Germany had won WWI, most of Europe would be economically dependent on the country.

84) To raise money for the war, allied governments issued war bonds. This was the first time many people were introduced to financial securities. In America, war bonds were called Liberty Bonds, and buying them was considered a patriotic duty.

"Defend your country with your dollars"

85) Britain joined the war partly because it feared both

outcomes of a war where it wasn't involved. If Germany and Austria-Hungary had won, Britain wouldn't have any friends left in Europe. If France and Russia had won, they wouldn't be too happy about Britain not helping out, and they would cut ties with the country. Either way, Britain would have lost respect around the world, especially in places like India and the Mediterranean (where it had many colonies). Therefore, Britain decided that it had no choice but to join.

86) **WWI** ended at 11 o'clock on 11th November, 1918.

87) There was a minimum height requirement for the British Army which was five foot three. Shorter men were recruited however, and a new role was created for them known as the 'Bantam Battalions'. This consisted of mining and tunnelling where their height was an advantage.

88) When the war started, Germany fought on two fronts. They invaded France (through Belgium) on the Western Front, and they fought Russia in the Eastern Front. Russia was never able to break through any of Germany's defense lines on the Eastern Front.

89) Russia's losses in the war caused serious problems back home. The war caused poverty, food scarcity, and economic instability. As a result, Russians revolted against Czar Nicolas II and ended his regime. They particularly disliked the Czar because his wife was born in Germany. Due to this Revolution, the country stopped participating in WWI in 1917.

90) President Woodrow Wilson went to congress and

declared war on Germany on April 2nd, 1917. This happened right after Germany sank four American merchant ships that were transporting supplies to Britain.

91) During WWI, Winston Churchill served in the military as First Lord of British Admiralty. He resigned from his post after a failed military campaign, and he took another post with a French battalion.

92) Italy joined the war on the side of the allied powers on May 23rd, 1915, when it declared war on Austria-Hungary.

93) The British Navy made a surprise attack on docked German vessels in early 1915. They hoped that Germans would be willing to confront them in a naval battle at the time, but Germany knew they had a weaker navy so they avoided conflicts at sea for that entire year.

94) Although planes were widely used in the war, they didn't make as much of an impact as British battleships and German submarines.

95) Britain created the Royal Air force on April 1st, 1918, becoming the first country in the world to have an air force that was independent of other branches of the military.

96) Germany launched its very last WWI offense on 15th July, 1918. This came to be known as the Second Battle of Marne.

97) WWI created the opportunity for Afghanistan to break away from British control and to become an independent country. Britain's resources were drained after the war, so

they readily gave in when Afghanistan pushed for independence.

98) The war heavily contributed to the spread of the Spanish flu that infected one-third of the world's population. Soldiers who returned to their home countries around the world spread the flu, which resulted in many more deaths than the actual war.

99) Unlike the tanks used today, those used in WWI were very crude. They were hard to drive, the inside was noisy, filled with smoke, and they didn't have shock absorbers which made the soldiers inside bounce around all the time. The soldiers who operated the tanks had to wear masks to protect their faces as enemy fire would produce sharp pieces of steel that would fly around inside. In the latter stages of WWI, Renault, the car company, designed a light tank that could be mass-produced. This gave France and the allied powers a great advantage, and contributed to their victory.

The British Mark V-star Tank

100) Britain caught many German spies on its soil during

the war. Eleven spies were executed at the Tower of London.

101) Before WWI, wrist watches were rare, and they were mostly worn by high-class women as jewellery. Men often carried pocket watches. Wristwatches became common during WWI because it was hard for men (mostly soldiers) to use pocket watches while fighting in the trenches.

102) Barbed wire was widely used during the war to protect the trenches, and to direct enemy soldiers towards "kill zones."

103) The term "crimes against humanity" was first used in a joint statement by allied forces in May 1915. In that statement, they rebuked the Ottoman Empire for killing more than half of all Armenian civilians, and they accused the Turks of committing crimes against humanity.

104) Trench coats got their name from WWI trenches. Although these kinds of coats existed before the war, they became popular during the war because they were specially designed and issued to British military officers, some of whom supervised the war in the trenches.

105) When the war started, the world was mostly powered by horses, as well as coal and steam engines. The nature of WWI forced the world to adopt the use of oil at a faster pace. Aircraft, submarines, tanks, and new battleships all used internal combustion engines, so the demand for oil increased.

106) A medical condition known as "trench foot" was very

common during the war. Soldiers wore tight boots in water-logged trenches for days or even weeks. Their legs would swell and rot, and even had to be cut off sometimes.

107) **WWI** caused one of the worst refugee crises in European history. It's estimated that more than 7.5 million people were displaced during the war.

Jewish refugees from Lublin, Poland, on the road to Austrian lines

108) Blood transfusions became popular during **WWI**. Although the procedure had been attempted a few times before the war, the modern techniques used to preserve blood, and to differentiate between blood types, were developed just as the war started.

109) Ireland broke away from Britain to become an independent country mostly because of events that played out during **WWI**. The UK and Ireland were sorting out governance issues in early 1914, but that was put on hold when the war broke out, which was very disappointing to the Irish people. Ireland also disliked Britain's decision to

draft Irishmen into the army. After WWI, Ireland declared independence and won.

110) Tunnel digging was one of the most feared jobs on the Western Front. Diggers were often killed by collapsing tunnel roofs, gas attacks, or explosives.

111) Guided missiles were first invented during WWI, but they were never actually used in the war because they failed to work accurately during tests.

112) Vegetarian sausages were invented during WWI by the mayor of Cologne as an alternative to meat, which was scarce and expensive at the time.

113) Mustard gas was first used as a chemical weapon in 1917. Unlike other gases, it was hard to detect, and it was very lethal.

114) WWI was the first war fought after the assembly line was perfected. As a result, industrial mass production changed the way the war was fought. Britain, Germany, and France all used assembly lines to produce munitions, tanks, vehicles, and planes in record high numbers.

115) President Woodrow Wilson came up with a fourteen point plan that would have ensured peace after the war, but he lacked the necessary political support both in America and Europe to execute that plan.

116) Palestine was part of the Ottoman Empire when WWI started. The allies promised the local Arab tribes that they could keep Palestinian land if they helped to fight the Turks. However, when the Ottoman Empire fell, Britain went back on its word and colonized Palestine.

Americans were unhappy with Britain's imperial ambitions, so Britain decided to establish a national home for the Jewish people in Palestine in order to appease the United States. Those events set the stage for the Middle-East conflict that persists to date.

117) Surgeons started wearing blue scrubs during WWI. Soldiers used to die in high numbers after surgery due to infections. A French doctor named Rene Leriche figured out that the infections could be prevented if the clothes used by surgeons were color-coded so that they wouldn't be mixed with other supplies during transportation. The practice was quickly adopted throughout France, and it rapidly spread to other countries.

118) WWI led to the nationalization of railways throughout Europe. Railways were very important during the war because they were used to transport soldiers and bulky supplies to the battlefront, and to move wounded soldiers away from the action. Governments in Europe had to take over all railway operations from smaller companies to ensure that the trains always ran uninterrupted.

En route to the front line

119) To help with the labor shortages during the war, France and Britain recruited 135,000 Chinese nationals and brought them over by sea to Europe. Some of them returned to China after the war, but others stayed and started Chinese communities in cities like Paris.

120) The common medical practice known as 'triage' started during WWI. During the war, doctors often dealt with a high number of injured patients at the same time, so they had to create a system that allowed them to prioritize patient treatment in a way that would increase the number of survivors. Triage is still used today in emergency rooms and during disasters.

121) Political cartoons and caricatures were very popular during WWI. Most pictures from the war were too horrifying to print on newspapers, so cartoons were used instead. Caricatures also came in handy as propaganda tools. For example, in Britain, allied soldiers were drawn as big and strong, while German soldiers were drawn as small, weak, or evil-looking.

Propaganda of Hitler & Tojo

122) The idea of daylight-savings time was proposed a few times before the war started, but it was first introduced in Germany in 1916 as a way to save energy and to make more use of daylight hours. Britain was the second country to introduce it just a few weeks after Germany. The US and France followed suit soon after.

123) When the United States joined WWI, it was so worried about German spies that it introduced the Espionage Act of 1917 and the Sedition Act of 1918. Some people were prosecuted under these Acts, just for speaking up against the war, and many were concerned that it would end Freedom of Speech. Fortunately, those two Acts were revised after the war, and people could criticize the government again without fear.

124) Aircraft carriers were first used in battle during WWI. Before the war, planes could take off from ship decks, but no one had figured out how to land them back

on the ships. For most of the war, Britain, France, Russia, and Germany used sea-planes that would land near the ship before they were dragged on-board using cranes. Towards the end of the war, Britain built two ships on which they could land their smaller fighters.

125) WWI gave way to the rise of communism in Russia. The death and famine that resulted from the war caused the resentment of the ruling class to boil over. The people had a revolution and the Bolshevik Party came into power and became the world's first socialist state in 1917. This led to the creation of the Soviet Union just a few years after the war.

126) Poppies became the remembrance symbol of WWI because of a poem called "In Flanders Fields", which was written by a Canadian surgeon named John McCrae during the war. At the end of the war, an American woman named Moina Michael started offering people imitation poppies to raise money for poor veterans, and her idea quickly spread throughout the world.

127) Metallic prosthetic limbs became popular as a result of WWI. Custom-made wooden prosthetic limbs existed before the war, but only the rich could afford to buy them. As many people lost their limbs during the war, the British government contracted a private company to supply artificial metal limbs to former servicemen.

128) WWI changed the way women dressed. Before the war, women wore hobble skirts (long skirts that narrowed around the ankles) and other clothes that looked luxurious but restricted free movement. But as the war went on,

women had to take up traditional male jobs, so they began wearing clothes that were more practical.

129) **WWI** cemented the position of the US as a world power. The US was already the biggest economy in the world by 1913. The war devastated European powers so much that even the victors (Britain and France) were left in debt. The US on the other hand, joined the war later, and none of the battles were fought on its soil, affecting them less severely. Their economy had ample time to grow as the war raged on. Russia, Britain, and France relied heavily on the US for financial support during the war, and they took loans from America in order to rebuild after the war.

130) **WWI** ushered in large-scale industrial production of food. Before the war, most people ate fresh foods, which they grew in their own farms or bought from farmers' markets. However, during the war, European countries had to figure out how to feed hundreds of thousands of soldiers in the trenches. Food processing factories started cropping up all over France, Britain, and many other countries. Canned foods, in particular, were produced in large quantities. After the war, processed foods became staples in all households.

131) **WWI** helped to forge Canada's identity as a nation in its own right. Canada joined the war as a British Dominion. Although it was still a British Dominion when the war ended, it had become more self-directed (it had its own scat at the League of Nations, and it technically had its own army), although it remained a part of the British Empire for another twelve years.

132) As America recruited soldiers for the war, many factories in northern States were left without workers, and this led to the migration of more than 500,000 African Americans from southern States to northern cities such as New York, Chicago, and Detroit. This led to cultural integration in America, and it set the stage for the civil rights movement.

133) After Germany was defeated, it lost its empire. Its colonies in Africa and Asia were taken away by Britain and France, West Prussia (a part of the former German Empire) was given to Poland, and Alsace-Lorraine (its most economically productive region) was given to France.

134) Grenades were first mass-produced during WWI. They were also modified to be rocket-launched for the first time during the war.

135) One of the worst rail disasters occurred in May of 1915 when a troop train carrying hundreds of men crashed into a stationary train. Minutes later another train crashed into the wreckage of the previous two trains and the whole site caught fire, killing over two hundred people.

136) Cuba's economy grew during WWI because of sugar exports to Europe. Before the war, Europe relied on France's beet crop for sugar production, but since the beet fields had become fighting grounds, sugar production suffered. In the first two years of the war, Cuba built a dozen sugar mills, which were mostly financed by American investors.

137) On Christmas 1914, British and German soldiers who had been fighting for months called an unofficial

cease-fire. They met halfway on no man's land, shook hands, and toasted to each others' good health. During that first year of the war, life was especially hard in the trenches on the Western Front. When Christmas came around, both sides were homesick, and they started singing hymns. Soon, they were taking turns listening to each others hymns. In Ypres (Belgium), foot soldiers at the frontlines called a truce, emerged from the trenches and even supposedly played a friendly soccer match.

138) During the war, a mine explosion killed 10,000 German soldiers. To date, this is still considered to be the deadliest non-nuclear explosion of all time.

139) As a result of WWI, New York overtook London as the leading financial center in the world. Before the war, London was the world's only financial center; it was at the heart of the greatest empire at the time, and the Sterling Pound was very stable and highly credible. But just a few months before the war started, American banks were, for the first time, allowed to open foreign branches outside the US, so they started providing services for major businesses in all continents. By the end of WWI, Britain was in debt, and American banks were financing trade across the world.

140) When WWI started, many heads of European dynasties were related by blood. King George V of Britain, Kaiser Wilhelm II of Germany, and Czar Nicholas II of Russia were all Queen Victoria's Grand-children. Those three monarchs were also distant relatives of the Belgian, Portuguese, and Bulgarian royal families. By the end of the war, most of Europe's royal dynasties

were kicked out of power, giving way to democratic leaders.

141) Germany used Zeppelin Airships to bomb several British cities, including London during WWI. The British town of Great Yarmouth was the first to be aerially bombarded by German Zeppelins. This happened on 19th January, 1915. Even though the airships moved slowly, they were hard to shoot down because they flew so high, beyond the reach of most British aircraft. Fortunately, the British developed the Sopwith Camel fighters which could shoot down the zeppelins. In total, the Germans dropped 280 tons of bombs in Britain during fifty three Zeppelin raids and deployed fifty two fixed wind airplane raids. They killed 1,413 civilians and wounded 3,409 more.

Zeppelin L 13

142) The British Royal Navy developed the first depth charges in the summer of 1916. This was an important game-changer in the war because, for the first time, they

were able to target and destroy German submarines which had been sinking most of their supply ships.

143) WWI caused a steel shortage and, as a result, many countries had to construct concrete ships.

144) More than 170 million rounds of shells were manufactured in Europe by the end of WWI.

145) Journalists were banned from the frontline during the war because most governments believed that reporting on the war would be beneficial to the enemy. Journalists who tried to report on the realities of war faced imprisonment or even execution.

146) A German navy captain named Karl Von Muller spared many civilian lives during WWI. He was ordered to sink allied merchant ships, which he did. However, on his own initiative, he would give passengers enough time to collect their belongings and to abandon the ships, before he would sink them.

147) The Pool of Peace in Belgium is one of the most well-known WWI memorials. Before the war, the Spanbroekmolen Windmill stood at that location for 300 years. In November 1914, the windmill was destroyed by Germans, and it became the site of many battles. The Germans held onto it, until June 1917, when the British exploded mines below the site, creating a crater, forty feet deep and 250 feet wide. The crater was filled with water, and it became the Pool of Peace.

148) Even though all fighting ceased by the end of 1918,

technically, WWI didn't officially end until June 28, 1919, when the treaty of Versailles was signed.

149) Different countries had different nicknames for the helmets that were issued to them during the war. British soldiers called them 'Tin Hats' or 'Tommy', while American soldiers called them 'Doughboy', and German soldiers called them 'Salad Bowls'.

150) Food prices were so high during the war that the British government had to fix maximum food prices to ensure that people could afford to eat. There were also serious fuel shortages in Britain during the war and newspapers constantly printed advisories on how to save fuel when cooking.

151) Arthur Zimmerman, German's Foreign Minister during WWI, wrote a telegram to Mexico asking the country to join the war, and promising them territories within US soil if Germany won. Britain intercepted the telegram, decoded it, and later shared it with the US. This helped to convince America to join the war.

152) A British diplomat and a military officer named Thomas Edward Lawrence played a key role in engineering the Arab Revolt against the Turks. In the west, he became known as Lawrence of Arabia because he adopted Arabian culture so much that he looked more like an Arab than an Englishman.

153) In response to food and supply shortages during WWI, the British government criminalized certain things that were part of everyday life during peacetime. People

weren't allowed to sell candy and chocolate, to throw rice at weddings, or to sell cattle or horses.

154) The women who worked in factories that manufactured TNT in Britain were exposed to the toxic substance, and they suffered from jaundice. As a result of the jaundice, their skin turned orange-yellow, and they were nicknamed 'canary girls' or 'munitionettes'. 25% of all the canary girls died as a direct result of the toxins they handled at work.

155) A Hungarian soldier was shot in the brain (the frontal lobe area) during WWI. He survived, but he was physically unable to fall asleep. He lived his whole life without ever sleeping again.

156) When Adolf Hitler was a young soldier during WWI, he used to have a full moustache. He was however ordered by a senior German official to reduce it so that he could properly wear a gas mask. That's how he ended up with his iconic partial moustache.

157) After WWI, so many German men had died, that only one-third of women in the country were able to find husbands.

158) A compassionate British soldier spared the life of a wounded German during WWI. That man turned out to be Adolf Hitler.

159) Some children even served in the military during WWI with the youngest soldier to serve being only eight years old.

160) British soldiers drank so much tea during WWI, that

at some point the military enforced rations of six pints of tea per soldier per day.

Soldiers having tea

161) Military commanders often sent orders to the battle-front by putting notes in capsules that were tied around dogs. The dogs would then run to the battlefront to deliver the orders.

162) As a result of WWI, the Women's Suffrage Movement in Britain was split into two. The Mainstream Suffragette Movement called for a ceasefire for the duration of the war (meaning they would not push for their demands until the war was over). The Radical Suffragette Movement chose to continue pushing for women's rights even during the war, and they even demanded that women in the military should be put in combat roles.

163) The war led to the empowerment of nationalists in British territories, especially after the concept of self-determination was introduced in Eastern Europe. The British Empire faced resistance in Ireland, Egypt, India, Palestine, and Iraq towards the end of WWI.

164) The Belgian royal family had a very hands-on approach during the war. The King personally led the Belgian Army in battle, the Queen became a nurse and attended to wounded soldiers, and the Prince, who was only fourteen at the time, joined the army and served as a private.

165) Spain stayed neutral throughout WWI. Towards the end of the war, it was the only country whose media could freely report on the influenza epidemic. Other countries restricted such reports to maintain morale during the war. As a result, people thought that the country was more adversely affected by the flu, so they named it the Spanish Flu.

166) A British POW (prisoner of war) was in a German prison camp when he heard that his mother was dying. He pleaded with the Germans to let him go home and see his mother one last time, promising that he would come back. The German Kaiser let him go, expecting to never see him again. However, after visiting his ailing mother, the soldier actually did return to the prison camp.

167) After English, German was the second most-spoken language in the US before WWI. In fact, many schools, and local governments considered German an official language. However, when the war broke out, the language was suppressed, German books were burned, and German newspapers were discontinued in America.

168) During cold nights in the trenches, British and French soldiers would make 'machine gun tea'. They would put water into their machine guns, and fire thou-

sands of rounds towards the German trenches. The water in the machine gun would boil in the process and the soldiers would then collect it and use it to brew tea.

169) The renowned French scientist Marie Curie tried to donate her Nobel Prize gold medals towards the war effort, but the French National Bank wouldn't take them.

170) RMS Olympic (a cruise liner and the sister ship to the Titanic) was the only civilian ship to ever destroy a German Submarine during WWI. The submarine tried to sink the Olympic, but the massive ship was able to ram into the submarine and sink it first.

171) Retired US president Teddy Roosevelt volunteered to join the army during WWI. His act of courage inspired many young men to sign up as well.

172) Germany used up all the rubber within its borders during the war. The post-war rubber shortages were so severe that Germans had to design bicycles with metal springs in place of rubber tires.

173) New Zealand, which was a British Dominion during WWI, raised an army of 100,000 soldiers who sailed to Europe to join the war. At the time, the country only had a population of 1 million, meaning that 10% of all New Zealanders fought in WWI.

174) During WWI, German submarines were such a serious threat, that at one point, the British Army tried to train seagulls to target the submarines, and to poop on their periscopes. This plan failed because unlike pigeons, seagulls couldn't be trained.

German U-boat UB 14 with its crew

175) The legendary magician Houdini was hired by the US Army to teach the troops magic skills that could help them survive the war (like how to escape if they were captured and chained).

176) People with eye cataracts were hired to help detect flashing beacons of UV light during WWI. Some cataract patients tend to be very sensitive to ultraviolet light, and this came in handy when the allies were trying to land planes in the dark without being seen by the Germans.

177) Sexually transmitted diseases were very common during the war. When allied troops went home after the war, over 1.5 million cases of gonorrhoea and syphilis were reported in Britain, America and France.

178) King Edward VIII, who was the Prince of Wales at the time, wanted to join the army, but the government wouldn't let him because they didn't want the heir to the throne dying in battle, or getting captured by the enemy. Edward VIII still visited the Western Front as often as he could, and he even earned the Military Cross for his

role in the war. He was very well-liked by WWI veterans.

179) A thousand of London's iconic double-decker busses were used in the frontlines of WWI, mostly to ferry nurses and wounded soldiers to and from the trenches.

180) During WWI, the American navy painted its ships in dazzle camouflage (complex patterns of geometrical shapes). This was meant to create an optical illusion that would make it hard for the enemy to estimate how far the ships were, how fast they were moving, and in what direction they were headed.

181) During WWI, German and Russian soldiers were battling it out when they were all attacked by a pack of wolves. They agreed to a temporary ceasefire so that they could all deal with the wolves first.

182) Censorship was widely practiced by the British Government during WWI. For example, when the British vessel HMS Audacious was sunk in October 1914, the British Press was barred from reporting the incident. British citizens only found out about it through rumours spread by passengers who had witnessed the incident while aboard a different ship.

183) When the war broke out, cavalry units (horse riders) were considered superior to guard units (soldiers who marched on foot). In fact, members of cavalry regiments held higher military ranks than guardsmen. However, armies on both sides of the conflict quickly realized that riding horses into the battlefield wasn't practical anymore because they could be mowed down by machine guns.

From that point on, horses were only used for transport, not for charging into battle. Mules and horses were more reliable than lorries and tanks when it came to moving munitions through harsh terrain up to the battlefront during WWI.

184) Before WWI, Germany had set up a robust horse breeding program all over its empire. In fact, all horses had to be registered every year, as if they were members of the military reserves. That way, it was easy for the German Army to find enough horses when they were needed for battle. Britain didn't have as many horses as Germany but it imported one million horses from America during WWI. It also brought in an unconfirmed number of horses from New Zealand. Soldiers on both sides of the war made improvised gas masks and nose plugs to protect their horses from gas attacks during WWI, but the horses would mistake the masks for feed bags and destroy them, and they would end up dying anyway. Just like humans, horses would also get shell shocked during the war. Soldiers discovered that poorly bred horses would react bravely to the sound of exploding artillery, while well-bred horses would react in a cowardly manner. Historians estimate that horse lives were more valuable than human lives at some point during the war. In 1917, men who fell in battle could be replaced with new soldiers, but horses were irreplaceable.

Bazentin Ridge 1916

185) The British Government capitalized on Germany's attacks on civilians in order to encourage its citizens to join the army. British propaganda posters were used to argue that it was better to face bullets at the battlefront than to stay at home and be killed by bombs.

186) The French decided to build a 'fake Paris' near the actual city in order to confuse German bombers during WWI. Germany had been sending bombers to British cities in the dead of night, and the French were concerned that the same would happen in their country, so they decided to build entire neighborhoods that were imitations of Paris. The plan was to design 'fake Paris' in such a way that German pilots couldn't tell the difference when it was dark.

187) Sixteen days before the ill-fated civilian vessel RMS Lusitania set sail from America to Britain, Germany published an article in the New York Times, warning that it would sink the ship if it sailed as planned. The warning was ignored, and in the end, 1,198 lives were lost.

188) Women joined the police force in Britain for the first time during WWI. Initially, their jobs involved monitoring

other women working in munitions factories and helping to maintain discipline among the ranks. They also served as safety inspectors in the factories. Soon, they started patrolling public areas (e.g. train stations) and after the war, they became permanent police officers. Similarly, the transport sector in Britain was mostly staffed by women during the war. They worked as drivers, ticket collectors, cleaners and porters.

189) During WWI, there were special laws put in place for British civilians in military courts if they broke special rules that were created to help the war effort. People who were caught wasting food, selling strong alcohol, opening pubs past curfew time, wasting food by feeding wild animals, etc., could be brought before a military court and sentenced.

190) After the start of WWI, British women pushed for their own uniformed service. The WAAC (Women's Army Auxiliary Corps) was established during WWI, in December 1916. This paved the way for the creation of the Women's Royal Navy in 1917 and the Women's Royal Air force in 1918. In total, more than 100,000 women served in the British Military by the end of WWI.

191) A female Scottish doctor named Elsie Inglis volunteered to join the army as a medic when the war started. The military officers found her offer amusing, and told her to: "go home and sit still." She founded the Scottish Women's Hospital, and later, she moved to Serbia to treat wounded soldiers.

192) Women's soccer became popular during WWI. For

the first time, women were working together in large numbers in factories, so they decided to engage in leisure activities that were previously reserved for men. Each munitions factory formed its own football team, and the matches drew massive crowds.

193) WWI trenches were layered. There were frontline trenches which were followed by two or more support trenches. They were linked by alleyways which were called communications trenches. Soldiers fought and kept watch in the frontline trenches. The support trenches were used to prepare food, treat wounded soldiers, and to store munitions.

194) Britain had limited detention policies during the war, where citizens of Germany, Austria, Hungary, and other "enemy" states had to register with the police and report to stations for regular checks. These people were also subject to several other restrictions. They couldn't travel, live in areas that were likely to be invaded, or own any equipment that could be used to spy on the British military.

195) During the war, the Maxim machine guns used in the trenches were operated by five people at a time. One man would sight the machine gun, the second man would fire, a third man would feed ammunition to the gun, and two others would go back and forth, bringing boxes of ammunition to the front and taking empty boxes away.

Firing a Maxim gun at an aeroplane

196) Artillery guns were never placed at the frontline trench. They were actually placed behind the second trench line (also known as the first support trench), meaning that they fired shells over the heads of soldiers. This contributed to a higher rate of shellshock among soldiers on both sides of the war.

197) The German public didn't always support the war. In fact, in 1918, citizens started demonstrating and striking, calling an end to the war. Many of them were starving and their economy was a mess, so they didn't see the benefit of being at war.

198) Despite the grim nature of WWI, nine out of ten British soldiers actually survived the war.

199) The British army had many 'pals' battalions' during WWI. These were battalions that were made up almost entirely of people who came from a small geographical area (same town, same place of work, etc.). Many soldiers joined such battalions because they didn't want their friends, neighbors, or former colleagues to think less of them.

200) Most British military personnel were posted outside Britain when WWI started. They were mostly tasked with keeping order in the territories of the vast British Empire (including India and the African and Asian Colonies).

201) Army generals were actually banned from fighting during the war. Before WWI, generals would ride into battle with their men, and this showed that they were brave and capable leaders. However, with the widespread use of machine guns, the military didn't want to put highly experienced generals at the battlefront because they didn't want to lose good strategists.

202) Plastic surgery was first introduced during WWI. Surgeons started using skin grafts to repair the faces of victims who had suffered serious facial injuries.

203) In the years leading up to the war, Britain had a 'Two-Power Standard' for its naval fleet (which was the best in the world at that time). Under this standard, the Royal Navy was required to have a number of battleships whose collective strength was at least, equal to the combined strength of the second and third strongest navies in the world (which were France and Russia).

204) Two billion letters and an additional 114 million parcels were sent through the Royal Mail Service during the war. On average, twelve million letters were sent and delivered to and from the front every single week. Letters were the primary form of long-distance communication at the time, and the British army believed that keeping in touch with family members boosted soldiers' morale.

205) In the days leading up to the war, there was wide-

spread public unrest in Britain (and even more so in Ireland). Suffrage and labor movements were initially opposed to the war. However, most movements quickly rallied behind the government, when it became clear that winning the war was a matter of national pride.

206) During WWI, Britain was in 'total war' for the first time in its history. Total war meant that all public resources (both civilian and military) were directed towards fighting the enemy. It also meant that civilians could be ordered by the government to do certain things to support the war effort. For example, private steel millers were required to work for the government to make weapons.

207) Britain had a special 'war cabinet' during WWI. Its function was to make sure that government resources were utilized efficiently during the war, and that the war effort wasn't undermined by endless administrative red tape.

208) Motorized ambulances were created during the first war out of necessity and thousands volunteered to be drivers, including the famous Walt Disney.

WWI field ambulance vehicle

209) Catholic bishops were opposed to compulsory enlistment into the army, and they called for their church members to oppose the policy. This had a significant impact in Ireland (which was, and remains largely Catholic), and it may have contributed to the eventual withdrawal of Ireland from the UK.

210) WWI had a lasting effect on Britain's internal politics. The Conservative Party was credited with winning the war, while the liberal party was criticized for being indecisive (their leadership was seen as weak) during the war.

211) During peacetime, before the war, the British government only spent 13% of the country's GNP (Gross National Product), but the number increased greatly during the war, and by 1918, the government was spending up to 59% of Britain's GNP. Additionally, the government borrowed heavily, imposed heavy taxes, cancelled virtually all projects that weren't war-related, and diverted funds from other public services. Within the

duration of the war, British public debt rose from £625 million to £7.8 billion in less than five years.

212) In 1916, the government of Britain made it illegal for anyone dining in a public establishment to eat more than two courses for lunch and more than three courses for supper. Because times were hard, everyone was required to 'tighten their belts'.

213) The British royal family had to change its family name from 'The House of Saxe-Coburg and Gotha' to 'The House of Windsor' to appease the British public who were unhappy with the royal family's German ancestry. The British royals also dropped all their German titles and names and took up English surnames. German relatives of British royals who fought in the war had their titles stripped from them under the rules outlined in the Titles Deprivation Act of 1917. They were no longer considered to be in line for the British Crown.

214) By 1917, Britain consumed 827 million barrels of oil per year, most of which were shipped from the United States (and some from Mexico).

215) When the Russians revolted and overthrew Tsar Nicholas II, the Russian Government wanted him to be given asylum in Britain. The British cabinet agreed to offer the Tsar and his family asylum, but King George V (who was the Tsar's first cousin), felt that the public wouldn't like it, so he blocked the asylum offer. The Tsar and his family were later killed.

216) Most of the fighting during WWI occurred in Belgium, France, Luxembourg, and Alsace-Lorraine (a

part of modern-day France). These areas were at the heart of the war, although smaller related conflicts and resultant battles were spread across the world.

217) Germany officially joined WWI to back up Austria-Hungary, but behind the scenes, those in power saw the war as an opportunity to settle scores and disputes with other European powers (France, Russia, and Britain). Colonial disputes in Africa (and some parts of Asia) played a minor role in starting WWI. Although European powers had subdivided most of Africa and agreed on colonial boundaries, there were still some unresolved tensions because the Germans thought France and Britain had taken larger parts of the continent.

218) France had a big and war-ready army at the start of WWI because it had 'universal conscription'. Every year, men who were about to turn twenty one were enlisted into the army, and they served in active duty for three years before going into the reserves. It was therefore very easy for the French to mobilize a massive army on short notice because most able-bodied men were already trained, and they were either in active service or in the reserves.

219) In August 1914, after suffering a series of devastating losses, the French feared that Paris would fall, so they moved the government to Bordeaux.

220) The French had a tradition of firing or transferring Generals and Commanders-in-chief who lost in battle. This practice had mixed results during WWI. In some cases, it led to better performance, but in others, it led to greater losses.

221) In 1917, many in the French army had completely lost morale for the war. They had come to believe that their infantry units would never prevail against German artillery and superior machine guns. They believed that they were dying in vain, and France would fall anyway. Their greatest hope was the arrival of American soldiers. In the spring of 1917, over 35,000 French soldiers mutinied. Most of these cases were the result of disappointment and despair among the soldiers. Their latest offensive (the Neville offensive) had failed. They were expecting backup from American soldiers who had not shown up. The mutinies were kept secret for the remainder of the war, because the French government worried that these cases would spread.

222) During WWI, French soldiers fought in other theaters of war apart from the Western Front. France sent some soldiers to occupy German colonies in Cameroon and Togo, and others to fight against the Ottomans in Palestine and the Dardanelles. The French also used troops from their North African territories and other colonies to fight in secondary battles, so as to avoid diverting too many soldiers from the Western Front. These troops were used to fight in Romania and in the Balkans.

223) When Germany was defeated, the allies took away Cameroon, Togo, and Tanganyika as part of the post-war settlements.

224) Rifle designs remained the same throughout WWI because all countries were focused on improving their larger weapons (such as tanks and machine guns), and developing chemical weapons (poisonous gases).

Machine gun crew with gas masks

225) France suffered mass casualties at the start of WWI partly because they were trained to attack the enemy in mass formations, a strategy that was outdated by that time (because the Germans had machine guns). The fact that their soldiers wore blue uniforms that were easily visible by enemy soldiers, also didn't help.

226) The German homeland was safe for most of the war, with the exception of the East Prussia region, which was temporarily invaded by the Russians in 1914. Other than that, there were virtually no battles fought within Germany in the entire war.

227) The German monarchy had hoped that the war would unite people behind the Kaiser and lessen the public support for the Social Democrats (who were critical of the monarchy). This worked at first as the Social Democrats backed the Kaiser, but when the war took longer than expected, Germans became unhappy again. After their defeat, the Germans were discontent with their government, and they had a revolution between

1918 and 1919. As a result of the revolution, they kicked out their monarchs and embraced a stronger democratic system. As the war ended, the German Kaiser (and his heirs) stepped down from the throne and the Social Democratic Party formed a government. The German Empire fell, and it was replaced by the Weimar Republic.

228) In 1915, the German government massacred five million pigs in an incident that came to be known as 'Schweinemord'. The pigs were killed both for food, and as a way to reserve more grains (which were used as pig feed).

229) When the Belgians were invaded by the Germans (whose ultimate aim was to get to France), they resisted the invasion by fighting back and destroying their own railways to keep the Germans from advancing. Germans had expected to have an easy passage through Belgium, so they angrily reacted by killing 6,000 civilians.

230) After America declared war on Germany, some German generals didn't see it as much of a threat because they believed that Americans were fat, undisciplined, and unfamiliar with the hardships of prolonged severe fighting. They were however disappointed to discover that American soldiers were in good form and highly motivated to win the war.

231) In 1916, Germany implemented the Hindenburg Program, which required that all economic resources in the country be put towards the creation of weapons. Church bells, copper roofs, and many other metal installa-

tions were ripped out, taken to munitions factories, and used as raw materials.

232) In Germany, only soldiers who were permanently crippled could be discharged from the army. Wounded soldiers were sent back to the trenches as soon as they showed signs of recovery.

Wounded soldiers at Omaha Beach

233) Soldiers on both sides of the war were issued with rifles. British soldiers used the Lee-Enfield .303 bolt-action rifle during WWI and its standard magazine could hold ten bullets. It was a well-made weapon that performed well under the tough conditions in the trenches. German infantry soldiers used the Gewehr 98 rifle. It was well designed and fairly accurate, but it wasn't well suited for the trenches.

234) Machine guns were very important in determining the outcomes of many battles in WWI. The Germans used the Maschinengewehr 08, a variation of the original American Maxim machine gun. This gun could fire up to

400 rounds per minute. The British used the Vickers machine gun, which was also a Maxim machine gun variant. It could fire 450 to 500 rounds per minute.

235) There were many different types of artillery guns used during the war. Artillery was meant to 'soften up' enemy positions before the infantry teams could advance. The British used the Howitzer Mark 1, which could fire two shells a minute (each weighing 290 pounds/131kg). The Germans had the so-called 'Paris Gun' which they famously used to shell Paris from 75 miles (120 km) away. It could fire shells up to 25 miles (40 km) into the air. Most of the shells fired from the 'Paris gun' never actually hit the city, but they were so loud they scared many civilians into evacuating.

236) When WWI started, most armies had small planes with bodies made of wood and canvas. By the end of the war, they had highly sophisticated fighters like the German Fokker Eindecker and the British Sopwith Camel. Most historians agree that the aviation industry wouldn't have advanced so much in the early 20th century if WWI hadn't happened.

237) In response to Germans using U-boats (submarines) to sink merchant ships, the British built 'Q-Ships'. These were battleships that were disguised as merchant ships. They would wait for German submarines to emerge before shooting and destroying them. When German submarines switched to torpedoing merchant ships without emerging from the water, the British started using convoys to secure their supply ships. Battleships would

meet merchant ships at sea and escort them till they docked on British shores.

238) European powers that participated in WWI evaluated an estimated 3,000 chemicals for potential use as weapons. Of those, fifty were actually used on the battlefield.

239) In Flanders (a place in northern Belgium), it's esti-mated that one million miles (1.61 million kilometers) of barbed wire was used at the battlefront. That's enough barbed wire to circle the earth about forty times over.

240) The shells used during WWI were unreliable; a significant percentage would remain unexploded after being launched. It's estimated that there are still millions of unexploded WWI shells buried in the French country-side even today. Records show that every single year, bomb disposal units handle about forty tons of unexploded shells within the Verdun area of France alone.

241) Battlefield tactics evolved in many ways during WWI. For example, at the start of the war, commanders were in charge of companies with more than 100 men. By the end of the war, commanders were in charge of squads of about ten soldiers or so.

242) When Germans first used chlorine gas in battle, allied soldiers thought that it was just a smoke-screen meant to provide cover for German soldiers who were about to attack. They marched onward into the cloud of chlorine gas, and many of them were killed.

243) Poison gases proved to be very unreliable weapons

during the war. They were double-edged swords. Attackers who used the gas were often killed when the winds shifted and blew in the opposite direction. To deal with this problem, the Germans developed special artillery shells that could be used to deliver poison gas to enemy positions.

244) When the war started, generals would use motorcycle couriers to deliver orders from command stations to the battlefront. This method became ineffective because battle conditions would change so rapidly. They, therefore, changed tactics and started using mirrors and flashing lights to send orders in Morse code. In some cases, fast runners would deliver more detailed messages. As the war went on, both sides started using aircraft to drop messages from generals to the soldiers at the battlefront.

245) Both the allies and the Germans floated manned observation balloons above the trenches. The balloons were used as observation posts. They were manned by two soldiers who would observe enemy positions and send messages down to the artillery operators. Enemy planes would often try to shoot down the balloons, but they were protected by anti-aircraft guns on the ground.

Observation balloon ascending

246) In the early stages of WWI, pilots used to go up without any parachutes. That's mostly because the kinds of parachutes that were available at the time were too heavy to bring along. Britain was slow in developing lighter parachutes because they were concerned that if pilots had parachutes, they would become cowards and abandon their planes at the first sight of trouble.

247) Large bomber aircrafts were developed in the course of WWI. These bombers would fly deep into enemy territory and drop bombs on strategic sites (mostly supply bases). The bombers were slow easy targets, so they had to fly along with many fighter escorts for protection.

248) The Germans were the first to train and deploy snipers who used rifles with telescopic sights to shoot allied soldiers who exposed themselves in the trenches.

249) As European countries were taking sides at the start of the war, Spain's Prime Minister Eduardo Dato declared that Spain would remain neutral. This declaration was

made on August 7, 1914, and it stayed in place for the entire duration of the war.

250) Japan participated in WWI, in alliance with the allies (Britain, France, and Russia). Japan was tasked with securing shipping lanes in the Pacific and the Indian Ocean, to keep them from falling under the control of Germany. The Japanese had imperial ambitions during WWI and they saw the war as an opportunity to expand their influence in China and other Asian countries. Since Germany was busy fighting the war, Japan seized some German territories in and around Asia (e.g. Micronesia). Although Japan and the United States fought on the same side during WWI, there was a lot of tension between the two powers throughout that era. The US was opposed to Japan's ambitions to colonize Asian countries, and they even blocked Japan's plans to send 70,000 troops to occupy Siberia in 1918. Japan was also concerned about America's increasing influence in Asia.

ALSO BY SCOTT MATTHEWS

Check out our most popular title: '3666 Interesting, Fun And Crazy Facts You Won't Believe Are True'. Search for it on Amazon to get your copy today!

Did you enjoy the book or learn something new? It really helps out small publishers like French Hacking if you could leave a quick review on Amazon so others in the community can also find the book!

BONUS: 3666 INTERESTING, FUN AND CRAZY FACTS YOU WON'T BELIEVE ARE TRUE

1) It is false that you can bite through a finger as easily as a carrot. It takes 200 newtons to bite through a raw carrot and 1485 newtons just to cause a fracture to a finger.

2) It took over 22 centuries to complete the Great Wall of China. It was built, rebuilt and extended by many imperial dynasties and kingdoms. The wall exceeds 12,000 miles (20,000km).

3) The largest empire the world has ever seen was the British Empire which covered almost a quarter of the planet in its peak in 1920.

4) Most of the camels in Saudi Arabia are imported from Australia.

5) China produces the most pollution in the world contributing 30% of all the countries total. These come from coal, oil and natural gases.

6) There are currently 1.6 billion live websites on the web

right now. However 99% of these sites you cannot access through Google and is known as the Deep Web.

7) Just like all languages, sign language has different accents based on country, age, ethnicity and whether the person is deaf or not.

8) There are over 1200 different species of bats in the world and contrary to popular belief none of them are blind. Bats can hunt in the dark using echolocation, which means they use echoes of self-produced sounds bouncing off objects to help them navigate.

9) When you're buried six feet down in soil and without a coffin, an average adult body normally takes eight to twelve years to decompose to a skeleton.

10) Pigs are physically incapable to look up into the sky.

11) The largest detonated bomb in the world was the Tsar Bomba on October 30 in 1961 by the Soviet Union. The blast was 3,000 times stronger than the bomb used on Hiroshima. The impact was enough to break windows 560 miles (900km) away.

12) The wars between Romans and Persians lasted about 721 years, the longest conflict in human history.

13) There were at least forty two known assassination plots against Hitler.

14) It took approximately 75 years for the telephone to reach 50 million users, the radio 38 years, 13 years for the television, 4 for the Internet, 2 for Facebook and only 19 days for Pokemon Go.

15) The biggest island is the world is Greenland as Australia is a continent.

16) In 2018, 4 billion people have access to the internet yet 844 million people still don't have access to clean water.

17) A single teaspoon of water has eight times more atoms than there are teaspoons full of water in the Atlantic Ocean.

18) Ancient Egyptians used headrests made of stone instead of pillows.

19) France was the first country to introduce the registration plate on August 14th 1893.

20) The Netherlands was the first country to legalise same sex marriage which was in 2001.

21) The average human attention span has almost halved since 2,000 decreasing from 20 seconds to 12 in 2018.

22) The oldest recorded tree in the world is reported to be 9,550 years old located in Dalarna, Sweden.

23) The oldest living system ever recorded is the Cyanobacterias, a type of bacteria that originated 2.8 billion years ago.

24) Being hungry causes serotonin levels to drop, causing a whirlwind of uncontrollable emotions including anxiety, stress and anger.

25) On Monday March 23, 2178, Pluto will complete its full orbit since its original discovery in 1930.